MAKE IT WITH™
RECYCLABLES

Written by
Anna Llimós Plomer

Illustrated by
José María Casanova

BOOK HOUSE

This edition first published in MMXVII by
Book House

Distributed by Black Rabbit Books
P.O. Box 3263
Mankato
Minnesota MN 56002

Cataloging-in-Publication Data is available
from the Library of Congress

Printed in the United States
At Corporate Graphics,
North Mankato, Minnesota

9 8 7 6 5 4 3 2 1

ISBN: 978-1-911242-09-3

Contents

Introduction

Cardboard egg boxes and paper towel tubes; plastic cups, bottles, and frozen food containers; milk and juice cartons, cans, and polystyrene trays are all objects that people throw away every day. They are used to store food, to wrap gifts, to protect fragile objects and so on. However, most of these throwaway materials can be reused in other ways. The process of reusing items is called recycling.

A lot of trash can be recycled to make fun crafts. How many times have you had to go out and buy cartons, boxes, gift wrap, or other materials for your craft projects? Taking advantage of used supplies is a great way to develop your imagination as you give new shapes to objects that seemed to be useless. However, when you want to reuse items of trash, always make sure they are clean and undamaged.

This book will give you ideas for making original crafts. You can use a juice or milk carton to make a cow container for storing small objects; you can turn an egg box into a palm tree, or a plastic dessert pot into the nose of a baby bear. Each of this book's twelve fun-to-make projects will help you see the many possibilities for recycling items of trash. You can complete these crafts following the easy, illustrated, step-by-step instructions. Better yet, after looking at the projects and the materials they use, you can invent your own craft projects.

To make almost any creation with recycled items you will also need some basic supplies, including scissors, sticky tape, glue, string, colored pencils, paints, and felt-tip pens. Watch for extra instructions at the end of each project to try other great ideas. Sometimes making just one small change creates a very different result.

Remember!
Whenever you see this symbol, or when you are using scissors, ask an adult to help you.

seascape

You don't need an aquarium, or even a fishbowl, to surround yourself with sea life. This colorful scene is almost as good as the real thing.

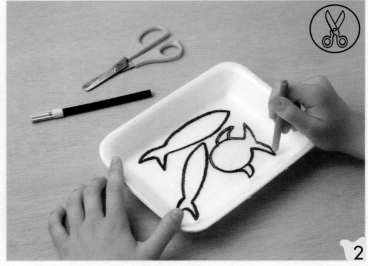

1 Tear light and dark blue tissue paper into small pieces. Dilute white glue with water. Brush the diluted glue onto each piece of tissue paper and lay it onto a polystyrene tray.

2 Use a black felt-tip pen to draw three fish on another tray. Indent the lines with a bradawl then cut them out.

Toolbox

You will need:
- scissors
- white glue
- paintbrushes
- 2 polystyrene trays
- black felt-tip pen
- bradawl (useful tool)
- light blue and dark blue tissue paper
- different colors of paint
- cocktail sticks

3 Paint each of the fish a different color and decorate them in different styles, such as stripes, spots, or swirls.

4 Stick a cocktail stick into the back of each fish, in the center.

5 Attach the fish onto the paper-covered tray (as shown) wherever you want them to be.

Move the fish around whenever you like— or make more fish so you can change your seascape!

Let your imagination soar!

Other ideas:
Make just one large shape, such as an octopus, and stick it into the center of the paper-covered tray.

Cow Container

Drink the juice, then turn the carton into this cute cow container.

Toolbox

You will need:
- colored pencils
- empty juice carton (large)
- thin white cardboard
- black felt-tip pen
- scissors
- glue stick
- bradawl
- string

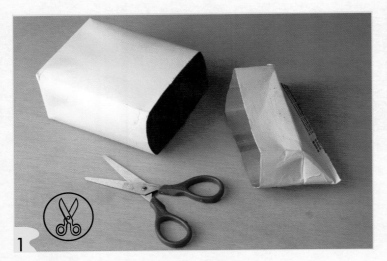

1 Use a pair of scissors to cut off the top of a clean, dry juice carton.

2 Cut a long piece of white cardboard about the same height as the carton. Draw black spots with a felt-tip pen and draw grass across the bottom with a green colored pencil.

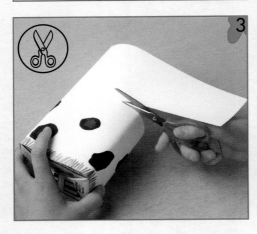

3 Wrap the drawing around the bottom of the carton and glue it on. Cut off any extra card.

4 On another piece of white cardboard, draw the front and back of a cow and cut out the shapes.

5 Color both parts of the cow using a black felt-tip pen and colored pencils.

6 Glue the front and back of the cow onto opposite sides of the carton.

Now put something special into your cow container.

7 Make a hole in the back of the cow with a bradawl. Thread a piece of string through the hole to make the cow's tail.

Let your imagination soar!

Other ideas:
Draw a lion or an elephant, or any other animal you like.

painted Palm

Cut up an egg box and make it into a palm tree. Painting the palm makes it look more lifelike.

Toolbox

You will need:
- scissors
- cardboard egg box (with a flat top)
- bradawl
- orange and green paints
- paintbrush
- thin, flexible wire

1 Cut off the cup-shaped parts of an egg box. Use a bradawl to poke a hole through the bottom of each cup, in the center.

2 Paint each egg cup orange.

3 Thread a piece of thin wire through the holes in the painted cups, alternating one cup downward, the next cup upward (you need enough wire to complete step 6).

4 Cut the top of the egg box lengthwise into seven strips. Make a hole with the bradawl at the end of each strip.

5 Paint the strips green to make the palm leaves.

6 Stick the wire through the hole in each green leaf, then twist the end of the wire to hold the leaves tightly in place.

You have made a beautiful palm tree and recycled a cardboard egg box that would otherwise have been thrown away.

Let your imagination soar!

Other ideas:
Make two hammock posts, each with three sections. Pin one end of a piece of netting material to the top of each.

11

Bottle Bowling

Make your own bowling game with a splash of paint, some labels, and six plastic bottles.

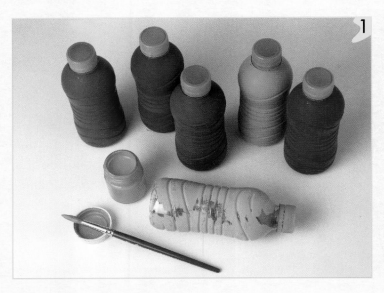

1. Paint each plastic bottle a different color. Use bright colors, such as red, yellow, blue, orange, purple, and green. Do not paint the bottle tops.

2. Cut six strips of white paper to make labels. Each strip should be long enough to fit around a bottle. Using colored pencils, draw a large number on each label.

Toolbox

You will need:
- different colored acrylic paint
- clear sticky tape
- 6 plastic bottles
- cardboard egg box
- colored pencils
- white paper
- paintbrush
- scissors

3. Use sticky tape to attach a paper label to each bottle.

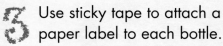

4 Soak the lower half of an egg box in water until it completely softens.

5 Make the egg box into a ball, squeezing it hard to remove as much water as possible so the ball holds together. Leave to dry.

6 Once the ball is completely dry, paint it green and decorate it with red and white spots.

Let your imagination soar!

Other ideas:
You can use modeling clay to make the ball, or use any small ball instead of making one.

Put the bowling pins in position... roll the ball... strike!

13

Movie Viewer

Show your own homemade films on this movie viewer. Playing with a cardboard box has never been more fun!

Toolbox

You will need:
- paintbrush
- light green paint
- medium-sized, long, thin rectangular box
- black felt-tip pen
- clear sticky tape
- bradawl
- two thin cardboard tubes
- colored pencils
- white paper
- ruler
- scissors

1 Paint the outside of a thin, rectangular box light green.

2 Using a black felt-tip pen and a ruler, draw a rectangle on the top side of the box. Leave a wide border. Make a hole with a bradawl and start cutting out a window.

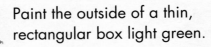

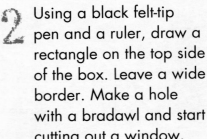

3 At each end of both sides of the box, draw a small circle around the end of your cardboard tube.

4 Use a bradawl to punch out the circles to make holes for the cardboard tubes.

5 Slot a cardboard tube through the holes. The tubes should stick out on each side of the box (as shown).

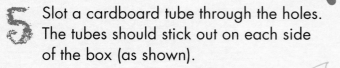

6 Cut a piece of white paper lengthwise as shown. Tape them together to make a long strip. It needs to be wider than the window.

Continues on next page…

7 Draw a series of pictures that tell a story along the length of the paper strip.

8 Color the drawings with colored pencils.

9 Open the box and place the paper strip inside, drawing side upward. Tape one end onto the cardboard tube.

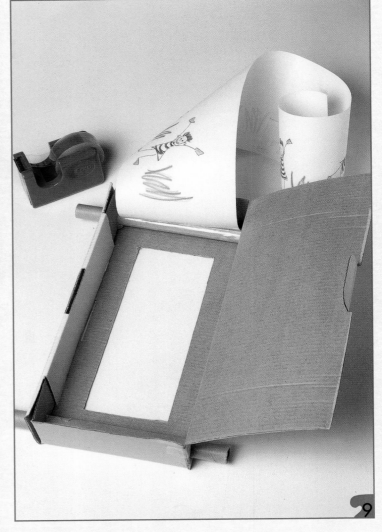

16

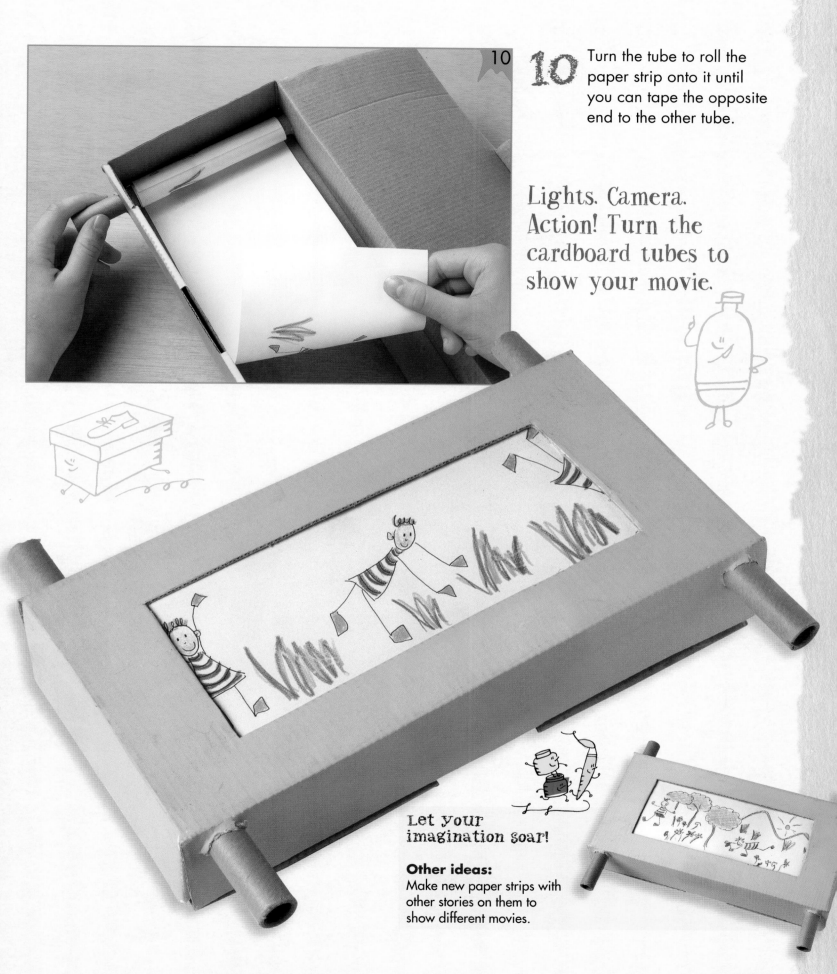

10 Turn the tube to roll the paper strip onto it until you can tape the opposite end to the other tube.

Lights. Camera. Action! Turn the cardboard tubes to show your movie.

Let your imagination soar!

Other ideas:
Make new paper strips with other stories on them to show different movies.

Simple Stampers

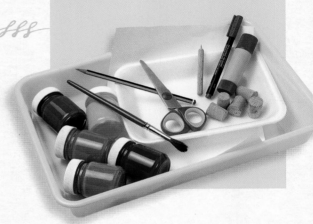

Making your own number stamps is as easy as counting 1, 2, 3, 4, 5. Five simple steps to make five simple stampers.

Toolbox

You will need:
- bradawl
- scissors
- polystyrene tray
- pencil
- glue stick
- 5 corks
- paintbrush
- different colors of poster paint
- white paper
- felt-tip pen

1 Cut out five squares from a polystyrene tray. (It is easier to cut if you indent the lines first with a bradawl). With a felt-tip pen, draw the numbers backward (use tracing paper) so they will print the right way round when stamped.

2 Go over each number with a pencil, pressing down hard to indent it. Decorate the edges of the squares by making small holes with a bradawl.

3 Use a glue stick to attach a cork to the back of each polystyrene square.

4 Use a different color for each stamp. Brush paint over the entire surface of the square and stamp out while the paint is still wet.

5 Stamp the numbers onto a piece of white paper.

Use your stamps on paper, wood, or cardboard. What you stamp is up to you!

Let your imagination soar!

Other ideas:
Draw flowers, boats, or whatever you like on your stamps instead of numbers.

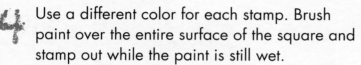

Cardboard Concertina

A round cardboard container is just the right thing for making this colorful little concertina.

1 Paint both parts of a round cardboard container red (inside and out). When dry, paint a decorative border of white triangles and green spots on the outsides of each part of the container.

2 Cut two strips of red paper, no wider than the inside of each container. Stick the strips together, end to end. Repeat this step with strips of green paper.

Toolbox

You will need:
- red, white, and green paints
- paintbrush
- round cardboard container
- scissors
- red and green paper
- ruler
- glue stick
- 2 corks
- clear glue

3 Now fold the red and green strips together. Place the end of one strip at right angles. Fold each strip on top of the next one. Repeat over and over, to make a concertina.

4 Glue one end of the concertina to the inside of each part of the container as shown.

5 Paint the two corks green.

Play your concertina by holding each end by its cork handle then opening and closing the two parts of the container.

6 Use clear glue to attach a cork to the center of each of the decorated ends of the container. The corks are the concertina's handles.

Let your imagination soar!

Other ideas:
Stand the closed concertina up on one of its corks and give it a spin. It becomes a spinning top.

21

Jumbo Jet

You can use the cardboard tube from a roll of paper towels to make this jet.

1 Draw the wings and tail shapes on a piece of cardboard then cut them out.

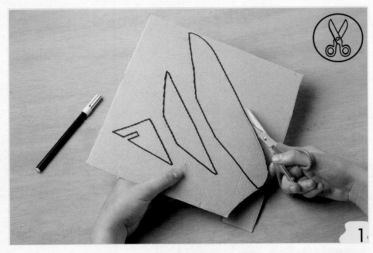

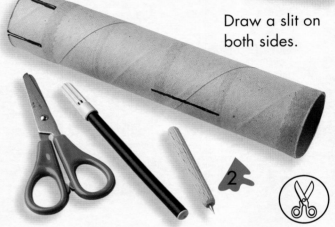

Draw a slit on both sides.

2 Draw lines on the cardboard tube to mark where to cut two slits for the wings and three for the tail. Cut along the lines, first with a bradawl, then with scissors.

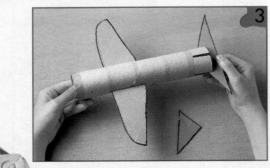

3 Slide the wings and tail pieces into the correct slits on the tube.

4 Cut one cup off a cardboard egg box.

5 Push the egg-box cup (open end first) into the front end of the cardboard tube so that most of it remains outside the tube.

6 Paint the whole plane yellow then decorate with green paint.

6

7 Paint the windows white with a black outline.

Your plane is ready to fly!

Let your imagination soar!

Other ideas:
Attach thread to the center of the tube to hang it from your bedroom ceiling.

Magic Hat

How can two people wear one hat at the same time?
Make this magic hat to learn the secret.

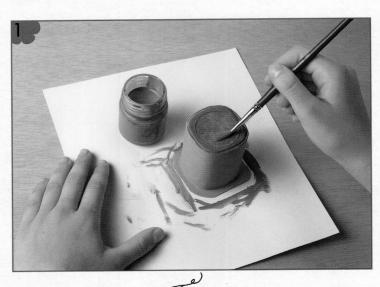

1 Paint the plastic yogurt pot green.

2 When the paint is dry, decorate the pot with white and red painted spots.

Toolbox

You will need:
- glue stick
- paintbrush
- plastic yogurt pot
- white paper
- cardboard tube (approx. 6in/15cm)
- black felt-tip pen
- colored pencils
- green, white, and red acrylic paints

3 Cut a piece of white paper just long enough to wrap around the tube. Draw two faces on it, as shown, with one face the right way up and the other upside down.

4 Wrap your drawing round the tube and use a glue stick to attach it.

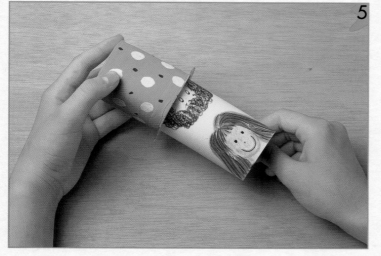

5 Put the yogurt pot over one end of the tube, covering one of the faces. The other face will now be wearing a spotty hat.

You can change the face wearing the hat—like magic! Just swap the hat to the opposite end of the tube.

Let your imagination soar!

Other ideas:
Cover the yogurt pot with decorated paper instead of painting it. If you put a sock over your hand, you can make it into a puppet. The sock becomes the puppet's body.

perfect purse

Make a lovely purse and help the environment, too.

Toolbox

You will need:
- empty juice carton
- scissors
- purple paper
- glue stick
- thin yellow cardboard
- black felt-tip pen
- green paint
- paintbrush
- clear sticky tape
- green plastic file divider
- self-adhesive Velcro

1 Cut the side off a large juice carton.

2 Wrap a strip of purple paper around the carton. Use a glue stick to attach the paper.

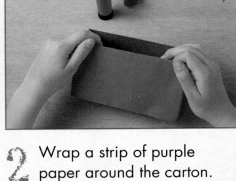

3 Draw a semicircle on thin yellow cardboard and cut it out. The diameter (width) of the semicircle should match the carton lengthwise.

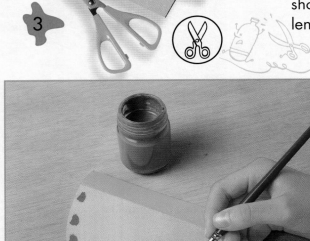

4 Paint green spots along the round edge to decorate it. This will be the flap for the purse.

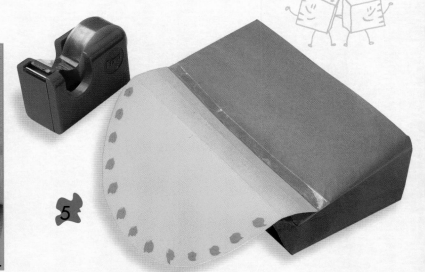

5 Stick the flap to the back of the carton with sticky tape so that it folds over the opening of the carton.

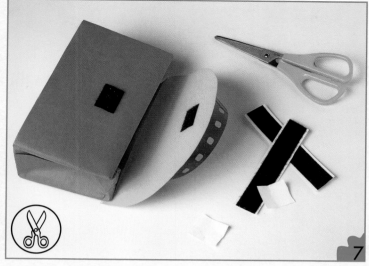

6 Make a handle for the purse. Cut the strip of holes off a plastic file and then attach the strip to the back of the purse with sticky tape.

7 Stick a small piece of self-adhesive Velcro to the front of the purse and to the inside of the flap to make a clasp.

You'll be surprised at how much you can carry in your handy purse.

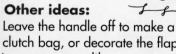

Let your imagination soar!

Other ideas:
Leave the handle off to make a clutch bag, or decorate the flap in any way you like.

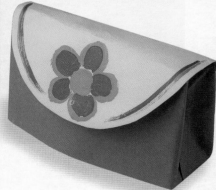

Baby Bear

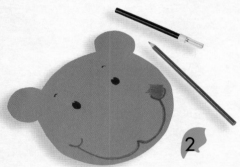

An empty chocolate dessert pot is just the thing to make a cute little nose for this baby bear's face.

1 Draw the shape of a bear's face and ears on orange cardboard and cut it out.

2 With a black felt-tip pen and a red colored pencil, draw on eyes, a mouth, and cheeks.

Toolbox

You will need:
- scissors
- glue stick
- black felt-tip pen
- thin orange card
- red colored pencil
- polystyrene tray
- brown plastic dessert pot
- clear glue

3 Draw shapes on a polystyrene tray and cut out. These should be smaller than the ears on the bear's face.

4

5

5 Trim the corners of the dessert pot with scissors. With clear glue, stick it in the center of the bear's face to make a 3D nose.

4 Stick the polystyrene ears on using a glue stick.

With its nose in a dessert pot, what little bear wouldn't have a big smile on its face?

Let your imagination soar!

Other ideas:
Use a different shape or color of plastic container to make the nose of another animal, such as a pig.

29

potted Flower

See how easily you can transform a plastic cup and a drinking straw into a decorative flower.

Toolbox

You will need:
- scissors
- paintbrush
- yellow, red, and green paint
- Popsicle sticks
- round plastic food container
  (such as an ice cream tub)
- clear glue
- red felt-tip pen
- yellow plastic file divider
- red plastic cup
- green paper
- clear sticky tape
- drinking straw
- bradawl

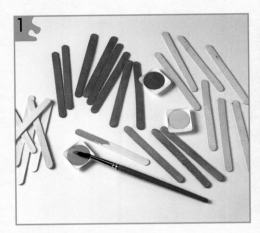

1 Gather enough Popsicle sticks to cover a round plastic container. Paint some of the sticks yellow, some red, and some green.

2 Use clear glue to attach the painted sticks to the outside of the container. Alternate the three colors as you glue them on.

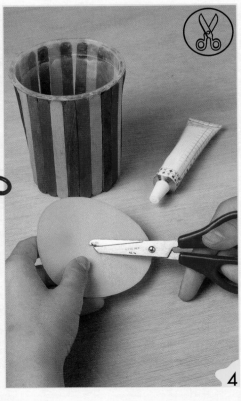

3 Using a red felt-tip pen, trace around the top of the container on to a yellow plastic file divider. Cut out the circle.

4 Make a small slit in the center of the circle with the bradawl. Glue the circle to the top of the container as if it were a cover.

5 Cut the sides of a red plastic cup into five equal strips. Trim the ends to make them rounded. Fold each strip outward, one at a time.

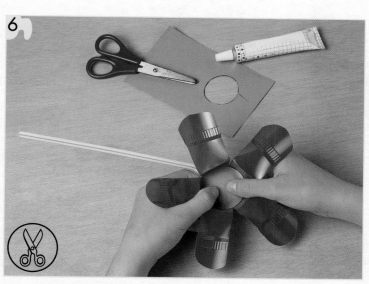

This flower is always in bloom and you never have to water it!

6 Cut a circle out of green paper and glue it to the bottom of the red cup to become the center of the flower.

7 Stick a drinking straw to the back of the flower with sticky tape to make the stem.

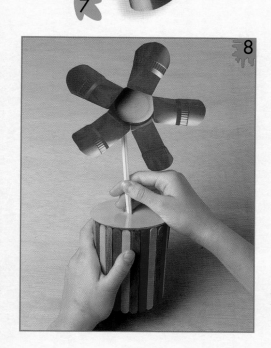

8 Push the end of the straw through the slit at the top of the flowerpot.

Let your imagination soar!

Other ideas:
Cut more slits into the cover to make a toothbrush holder. Put marbles or pebbles into the container before you cover it to stop it tipping over.

Notes for parents and teachers

Using recycled materials is a great way to develop a child's imagination. Everyday objects that are about to be thrown away can be used to make lovely craft projects. It is a good idea to collect lots of different kinds of materials and let children improvise with them.

The following suggestions can be an aid to making each project, and are a guide to the most appropriate age level for each one. It is important to point out that the suggested age level is based on the degree of difficulty of the process, but the projects can be easily adapted to various age levels.

p.6 **Seascape** When working with younger children it is advisable to use thin sheets of polystyrene. These are easier to cut than trays.
Ages 5 and up.

p.8 **Cow Container** To make the project easier, it can be painted with black and white acrylic paints instead of covering the carton with paper.
Ages 6 and up.

p.10 **Painted Palm** Instead of using wire, all the pieces can be stuck together with clear glue. A support can also be added in the shape of an island.
Ages 7 and up.

p.12 **Bottle Bowling** To make the bowling pins a little heavier, they can be partially filled with gravel or sand.
Ages 5 and up.

p.14 **Movie Viewer** This project is suitable for younger children if an adult can help to set up the "movie" on the tubes inside the box.
Ages 7 and up.

p.18 **Simple Stampers** By following the same steps and using fabric paints, the stamps can be used to print on T-shirts.
Ages 5 and up.

p.20 **Cardboard Concertina** This becomes a very simple spinning top project if the concertina paper folding part is left out.
Ages 6 and up.

p.22 **Jumbo Jet** If the egg box "cup" does not fit well into the end of the tube, stick it on with glue or sticky tape.
Ages 7 and up.

p.24 **Magic Hat** Before drawing the faces it is a good idea to place the hat on the tube so that you can mark where to start drawing.
Ages 5 and up.

p.26 **Perfect Purse** To make the bag even better, cover the carton with a piece of fabric, perhaps from an old item of clothing.
Ages 6 and up.

p.28 **Baby Bear** The bear's head could also be drawn on a sheet of polystyrene.
Ages 5 and up.

p.30 **Potted Flower** This project becomes much easier if the container is simply decorated using acrylic paints.
Ages 6 and up.